CEDAR CREST COLLEGE LIBRARY
ALLENTOWN, PA 18104-6196

THE TENNIS DRILL BOOK

Sharon Petro, MSA

University of Notre Dame

LEISURE PRESS

Champaign, Illinois

Library of Congress Cataloging-in-Publication Data

Petro, Sharon,
    The tennis drill book.

    1. Tennis.   2. Tennis—Training.   I. Title.
    GV995.P417   1986   796.342'07   84-47518
    ISBN 0-88011-224-7

Developmental Editor: Sue Ingels Mauck; Production Director: Ernie Noa; Type-
setter: Brad Colson; Text Design: Julie Szamocki; Text Layout: Janet Davenport;
Illustrated By: Mary Yemma Long; Cover Design and Layout: Julie Szamocki;
Printed By: United Graphics; Cover Photo: Raymond F. Patnaude, Jr.; Interior
Photos: Used with permission. From Groppel, J. L. (1984). *Tennis for advanced
players*. Champaign, IL: Human Kinetics.

ISBN: 0-88011-224-7

Copyright © 1986 by Sharon Petro

All rights reserved. Except for use in a review, the reproduction or utilization of this
work in any form or by any electronic, mechanical, or other means, now known or
hereafter invented, including xerography, photocopying, and recording, and in any
information storage and retrieval system, is forbidden without the written permission of the publisher.

Printed in the United States of America   10   9   8

Leisure Press
A Division of Human Kinetics
Web site: http://www.humankinetics.com

United States: Human Kinetics, P.O. Box 5076, Champaign, IL 61825-5076
1-800-747-4457
e-mail: humank@hkusa.com

Canada: Human Kinetics, Box 24040, Windsor, ON N8Y 4Y9
1-800-465-7301 (in Canada only)
e-mail: humank@hkcanada.com

Europe: Human Kinetics, P.O. Box IW14, Leeds LS16 6TR, United Kingdom
(44) 1132 781708
e-mail: humank@hkeurope.com

Australia: Human Kinetics, 57A Price Avenue, Lower Mitcham, South Australia 5062
(08) 277 1555
e-mail: humank@hkaustralia.com

New Zealand: Human Kinetics, P.O. Box 105-231, Auckland 1
(09) 523 3462
e-mail: humank@hknewz.com

Contents

1   Groundstroke Drills   1

2   Midcourt Drills   23

3 Volley Drills 35

4 Serve And Service Return Drills 61

5 Lob And Overhead Drills 77

6 Drills For Singles And Doubles Play 89

7 Footwork And Conditioning Drills 99

Dedication

To my parents
Louis and Jennie Petro
for their continual love and support

To my friend
Jan Schlaff
my source of confidence

To my teacher
Sylvia McCann
who provided a most important coaching model

Acknowledgments

I wish to extend a great deal of thanks to:

The many coaches who, over the years, have generously shared their knowledge and skill.

Linda Bunker, for giving me this opportunity.

Greta Roemer, Karen Grummell, and Jane Mullen, for the time they took in their thorough and creative critique of the manuscript.

Jackie Haslett and Carole Martin, for the many hours of typing and continued interest and support in this project.

Ray and Chris Patnaude, for their time and artistic talents in photography.

All of my Notre Dame tennis players for their patience.

Introduction

The One, Two, Three of Tennis

This collection of drills is not a "how to" book. It is not meant to teach you how to stand, how to grip the racket, or how to hit a tennis ball. Nor is it a book of tennis strategy. Your best resource for fulfilling these needs is a good teacher. To start on the right foot, you need to begin with a qualified professional who not only will teach you the fundamentals of tennis, but will take an interest in helping you to improve your game.

But don't stop there. Mastery of tennis is acquired through a three-step process: instruction, practice, and competition. None of the steps can be omitted. So follow your lessons with drilling. This will give you the opportunity to practice and strengthen the skills you have been taught. Then test those skills by playing competitive matches. The drills in this book are designed to help you make the transition from lessons to matchplay. But, just as the concert pianist must practice every day, the tennis player must drill regularly.

Drilling

Drilling is both challenging and fun. It falls between casual hitting and matchplay. It is more highly structured than informal practice, yet lacks the pressure of formal competition, so players are willing to try a greater variety of shots. This is important because even in casual practice, most of us rely on our stronger strokes. This makes us look more impressive and temporarily allows us to feel good about our game. But consequently, our good strokes get better while our weak ones never develop; then we wonder why we can't hit a backhand or an approach shot when we need one in a match. Drilling provides the opportunity to isolate the parts of our game that need the most attention and to concentrate on our weakest strokes.

For practicing any stroke, drilling is much more efficient than matchplay. In a match, the individual player spends only twenty-five percent of the total time actually hitting the ball. The rest of the time is spent chasing the ball, switching sides of the court, talking with the opponent, and so on. By the way, how many approach shots do you think you hit in that half-hour of actual hitting time during a two-hour match?

Drilling will also help you become acquainted with the court so that you will feel comfortable on all sections of the tennis court. The midcourt is the most commonly neglected area. We spend hours practicing groundstrokes from the baseline and volleys at the net, but rarely practice in that "no man's land" between the baseline and the net. We know that the doubles team that can take charge of the net will be the winning team, but we forget that the most difficult aspect of playing at the net is getting there. Plenty of practice in the midcourt and practice in developing the half volley are essential for playing at the net. Drilling will give you that practice.

In addition, drilling allows players of different skill levels to work together and receive mutual benefits. Your drill partner is an important person. You need a partner who is willing to help you become a better player by offering a challenge. (Your partner should push you, but not kill you!) In turn, you should be willing to do the same for your partner.

Drilling allows players, coaches, and instructors to structure practice time efficiently and gain the greatest possible benefits from that practice. Any tennis player *can* drill, and every player, from beginner to champion, *should* drill.

Stretching and Warming Up

Stretching is an important part of our physical activity that is too often neglected. Much of our childhood flexibility is lost because we don't stretch frequently. Many aches and pains, even injuries, sustained by the weekend athlete are caused by the loss of flexibility. Take ten to fifteen minutes every day to stretch. If not every day, at least take ten minutes before stepping onto the court to stretch your legs, back, arms, and shoulders. Remember to relax as you hold your stretched position for a slow count of thirty. Do not stretch to the point of pain, and never bounce. I also recommend that you stretch immediately after playing as you cool down. Try it, it feels good.

Most tennis players start warming up at the baseline and then move in closer to hit volleys at the net. But how often do you think the baseball player throws his first warm-up ball from centerfield to home plate? Our bodies need to start with small, controlled movements rather than large, powerful movements. I recommend that you start your warm-up at the net. Hit ten consecutive volleys and move back to the service line and hit ten shots. Then move to mid backcourt for ten more. Now you are ready to move back to the baseline for the deep, harder-hit shots. When it is time to warm up your arm and shoulder to serve, don't begin with your fastest serve. Start slow and easy to avoid straining your body. Following these tips will enable you to make a smooth transition from inactivity to strenuous activity.

Presentation of Material

For consistency, the following drill procedures are written for the right-handed player. I apologize to the many left-handed players who will use this collection, but soon we will have our day in the sun.

The drills are grouped according to the primary stroke they are designed to develop—the *volley*, the *half volley*, the *overhead*, and others. Within each group, the drills are arranged from the easiest to the most difficult.

Each drill identifies the number of players per court and the skill level for which it is most appropriate. Time limits are also suggested. But these are only guidelines. Be creative and flexible with them. Change time limits, target areas, and goals to create a challenge. Adapt the drills to your particular situation. Group drills, for example, can be played by as few as two players; many of the individual drills can be played by groups.

Some Practical Suggestions

Too often when players practice serving, the partner stands by, idly waiting for the balls to collect, and misses the opportunity to practice a most essential stroke—the service return. For maximum efficiency, make this standard procedure. Always practice the service return when your partner is practicing the serve.

One of the best partners a tennis player can have, but usually neglects, is the wall. It doesn't talk back and it always returns the ball. Many clubs now have practice lanes and ball machines available. Make use of them, they're a great way to perfect strokes.

To increase efficiency, keep a number of balls on hand for drilling so you won't have to waste time chasing and picking them up. Don't throw away those tired balls that are no longer suitable for competition. Collect them in a laundry basket or grocery bag and use them for drilling. Save your empty ball cans too, and use them for small targets to help sharpen your accuracy.

It's time to start now. Your teacher can only do so much. The rest is up to you. It takes a lot of practice to become a better player. It is my hope that this collection of drills will assist you on your journey to that goal. Have fun!

NOTE—In the tennis court diagrams that accompany the drills, the solid arrow (———→) indicates the path of the player and the broken arrow (- - - - →) indicates the path of the ball.

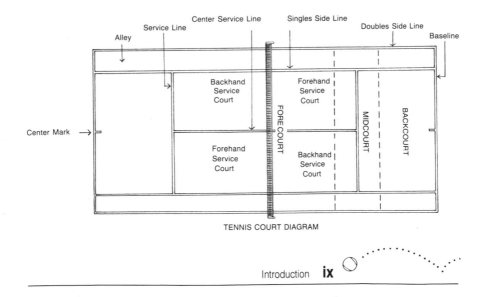

TENNIS COURT DIAGRAM

Summary of Primary and Secondary Skill Emphasis

Skill Emphasis	Drill Number
Approach shot	5, 24, 27, 28, 29, 30, 101
Conditioning	12, 13, 17, 23, 24, 70, 88, 89, 90, 91, 92, 93, 94, 95, 96, 100, 101, 102
Doubles	47, 48, 49, 56, 58, 60, 64, 65, 76, 77, 78, 83, 84, 85, 86, 87
Drop Shot	25
Footwork	1, 4, 8, 12, 24, 91, 95, 96, 97, 98, 99, 102, 103
Groundstroke	1, 2, 3, 4, 5, 6, 7, 8, 9, 10, 11, 12, 13, 14, 15, 16, 17, 18, 19, 20, 22, 26, 27, 34, 40, 41, 47, 80, 84, 85, 87, 98, 101, 102
Half Volley	14, 21, 22, 23, 37, 57, 75
Lob	60, 68, 69, 71, 72, 73, 74, 75, 76, 84, 101, 102
Overhead	30, 67, 70, 71, 72, 73, 74, 75, 76, 84, 101, 102
Serve	48, 49, 52, 53, 54, 55, 56, 57, 58, 59, 60, 61, 62, 63, 64, 65, 66
Service Return	48, 49, 58, 59, 60, 61, 62, 63, 64, 65, 66
Singles	15, 56, 77, 78, 79, 80, 81, 82
Volley	8, 14, 18, 21, 22, 23, 27, 29, 30, 31, 32, 33, 34, 35, 36, 37, 38, 39, 40, 41, 42, 43, 44, 45, 46, 47, 48, 49, 50, 51, 57, 58, 59, 71, 75, 84, 85, 86, 87, 100, 101, 102, 103

1 Groundstroke Drills

1. Groundstroke Shadow Drill

Emphasis: Groundstroke, Footwork
Skill level: Beginner
Players/court: 1 to Group

Purpose: To develop proper technique of forehand and backhand groundstrokes without the distraction of the ball and opponent.

Procedure: From the ready position, complete twenty forehand swings. Take time to check the grip, footwork, backswing, contact zone, follow-through, and recovery to the ready position. Follow the same procedure to complete twenty backhand swings. Then complete twenty swings alternating forehand and backhand.

Variation: Move and swing. Using shuffle steps, move to the right, left, up, and back to get the imaginary ball.

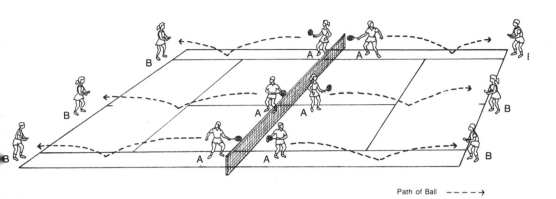

Path of Ball   ‒ ‒ ‒ ‒ →

2.   Drop Hit To Partner

Emphasis: Groundstroke
Skill level: Beginner
Players/court: 2 or Group

Purpose: To develop control and accuracy with the forehand and backhand groundstrokes.

Procedure: The hitters (A), with their backs to the net, drop hit to their partners (B), who are standing with their backs to the fence. B rolls the balls back to A. After six forehands and six backhands have been hit, players rotate.

NOTE—Hitters toss balls up and away from their bodies. This allows more time to prepare and gives them room to step into the swing. Caution the hitters not to endanger their partners by hitting too hard.

3. Hitting Tossed Ball To Partner

Emphasis: Groundstroke
Skill level: Beginner
Players/court: 2 or Group

Purpose: To develop control, accuracy, and timing with the forehand and backhand groundstrokes.

Procedure: The hitters (A) have their backs to the net facing their partners (B) who have their backs to the fence. The partners toss the ball to the hitters' forehand side, and the ball is hit with control back to the partner. After six forehands have been hit, the partners toss the ball to the backhand side. After six backhands have been hit, players rotate.

NOTE—Make clear to the partners that they should make the task as easy as possible for the hitters. You might suggest an underhand toss. Caution the hitters not to endanger their partners by hitting too hard.

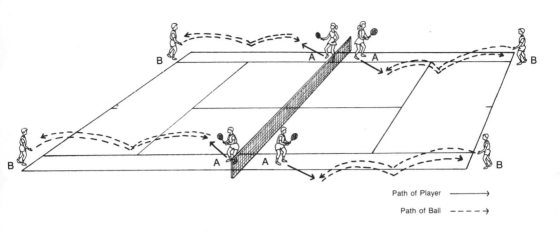

Path of Player ─────→
Path of Ball ─ ─ ─ ─→

4. Move and Hit

Emphasis: Groundstroke, Footwork
Skill level: Beginner
Players/court: 2 or group

Purpose: To develop the ability to run to a tossed ball and hit it with control and accuracy.

Procedure: The hitters (A) have their backs to the net facing their partners (B) who have their backs to the fence. The partners toss the ball to the forehand side, forcing the hitters to move to the ball with a few steps. The hitters hit the ball (with control) to the partners. After six forehands have been hit, the partners toss the ball to the backhand side. After six backhands have been hit, players rotate.

NOTE—As players feel comfortable with moving to the ball, forward and backward movement can be added to lateral movement.

5. 1, 2, 3, 4 Groundstrokes

Emphasis: Groundstroke, Approach
Skill level: Beginner, Intermediate, Advanced
Players/court: Group

Purpose: To develop deep groundstrokes.

Procedure: For beginners, Player A stands at the service line and B stands midway between the service line and baseline. Player A feeds a midcourt shot to B's forehand. B attempts to return the ball deep into the court. The court is divided into four quarters, each having a point value from one to four. A ball hopper placed in each corner is worth ten points if hit. A feeds five forehands, then five backhands. After twenty balls are hit, players rotate.

Variations:
1. As the skill level increases, A and B move back to the baseline. The ten-point target may be reduced in size to a ball can.
2. More advanced players can be fed running forehands and backhands. B starts in one corner and the ball is fed to the other corner.
3. The players can be limited to down-the-line or crosscourt shots.
4. The deep approach shot can be practiced with this method.

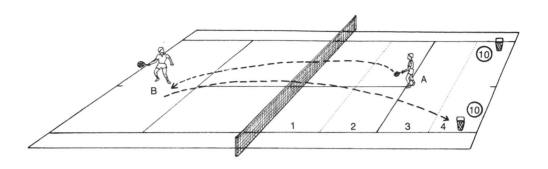

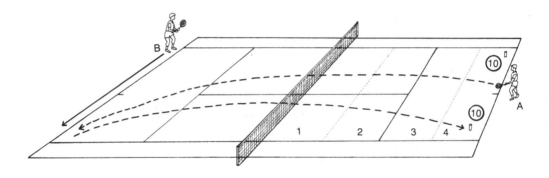

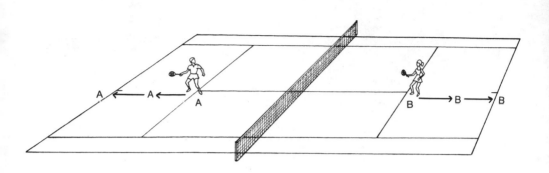

6. Ten to Move

Emphasis: Groundstroke
Skill level: Beginner, Intermediate, Advanced
Players/court: 2

Purpose: To develop controlled groundstrokes and to provide a warm-up.

Procedure: Players A and B start at the service line. Putting the ball in play with a drop hit, they must keep the ball in play for ten consecutive hits. The players then move back midway between the service line and the baseline. After completing ten consecutive hits, they move to the baseline to hit ten more.

7. Around The World

Emphasis: Groundstroke
Skill level: Beginner, Intermediate, Advanced
Players/court: Group

Purpose: To improve controlled hitting.

Procedure: Players form two lines at each baseline. Player A drop hits the ball to B and then runs around the court to the end of the opposite line. After returning the ball, B runs around the court to the end of the opposite line. The players keep a rally going as long as possible. Counting the consecutive hits aloud, they can strive for a set goal or compete with another group on an adjacent court.

Variations:
1. Each time someone misses, that player receives a letter of a predetermined word, such as TENNIS. When a player receives all of the letters of that word, the player is out. Play until there is a winner.
2. For more skillful players, limit the boundary to the backcourt, between the service line and baseline.
3. When someone misses, that player drops out and keeps busy with a conditioning activity (jump rope, sit-ups, etc.) until the next player misses. The first player then rejoins the group.

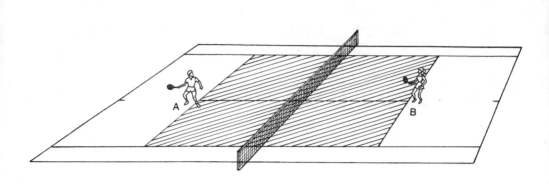

8. Short Game

Emphasis: Groundstroke, Volley, Footwork
Skill level: Beginner, Intermediate, Advanced
Players/court: 2

Purpose: To develop drop shot, volley and footwork.

Procedure: Play points using the service line and the singles sideline as boundaries. The point is started standing behind the service line with a drop hit into the diagonal service court. Switch courts on each point. A serves five points, then B serves five points. Play twenty points. If there is a tie, the player winning the tying point has the choice of service or court.

9. Keep It Deep

Emphasis: Groundstroke
Skill level: Intermediate, Advanced
Players/court: 2

Purpose: To develop deep consistent groundstrokes.

Procedure: Both players are at the baseline. The court boundaries are the baseline, singles sideline, and service line. Player A puts the ball into play with a drop hit from the forehand court. It must land deep in B's forehand court. B returns the ball to anywhere in the backcourt. The point is played out, ending when either player hits out of bounds. Player A begins the next point from the backhand court, to land deep in B's backhand court. Players keep score as usual. B "serves" the next game.

Variation: Target area could be made smaller for players with greater skill.

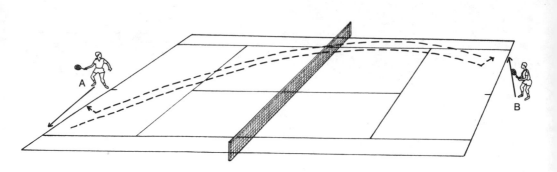

10. Crosscourt Rally

Emphasis: Groundstroke
Skill level: Intermediate, Advanced
Players/court: 2 or 4

Purpose: To develop placement of groundstrokes.

Procedure: Both players start in the middle of their baseline. Players attempt to keep a rally going with deep crosscourt forehands. After five minutes, players hit crosscourt backhands, trying to keep the ball deep in the backcourt.

Variation: Advanced players hit crosscourt, alternating forehands and backhands.

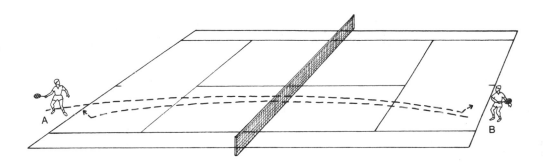

11. Down-The-Line Rally

Emphasis: Groundstroke
Skill level: Intermediate, Advanced
Players/court: 2 or 4

Purpose: To develop placement of groundstrokes.

Procedure: Both players stand to one side of the center mark at the baseline. Players attempt to keep a rally going down-the-line, A hitting forehands and B hitting backhands. After five minutes, players move to the other side of the court, A hitting backhands and B hitting forehands. Players should keep the ball deep in the backcourt.

12. Two-On-One At Baseline

Emphasis: Groundstroke, Conditioning, Footwork
Skill level: Intermediate, Advanced
Players/court: 3

Purpose: To develop placement of groundstrokes.

Procedure: All three players are at the baseline. A hits down-the-line to C's backhand. C returns crosscourt to B. B hits down-the-line to C's forehand corner. C moves to return the ball crosscourt to A, and the pattern continues. After five minutes, players rotate.

13. Down-The-Line And Crosscourt

Emphasis: Groundstroke, Conditioning, Footwork
Skill level: Intermediate, Advanced
Players/court: 2

Purpose: To develop placement of groundstrokes.

Procedure: Both players are at the baseline. Player A hits deep down-the-line. B returns deep crosscourt. A moves to the opposite corner and returns deep down-the-line. B moves to return deep crosscourt. The players continue this pattern. After five minutes, A hits crosscourt and B hits down-the-line.

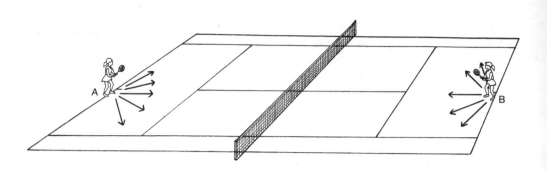

14.　Toe The Mark

Emphasis:　Groundstroke, Volley, Half Volley
Skill level:　Intermediate, Advanced
Players/court:　2

Purpose:　To develop an aggressive game.

Procedure:　Players rally with their toes on the baseline. The only time they can leave the baseline is to move in closer to the net. They are not allowed to move backwards behind the baseline.

NOTE—In order to develop an aggressive, offensive game, a player must learn to play the ball on the rise. Too often players stand far behind the baseline to hit balls that bounce well inside the baseline. This drill encourages hitting the ball on the rise and puts the player in a better position to move in to the net.

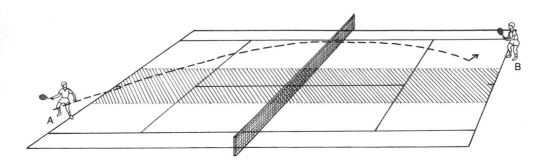

15. Three-Lane Game

Emphasis: Groundstroke, Singles
Skill level: Intermediate, Advanced
Players/court: 2

Purpose: To develop down-the-line and crosscourt shots to keep the opponent moving.

Procedure: The singles court is divided into three lanes as shown. The center lane is out of bounds. Both players start at the baseline. Player A drop hits the ball to start the point. A's "serve" must land in B's forehand lane. B can return the ball anywhere in either of the two outer lanes. Players play out the point. A's next "serve" must land in B's backhand lane. Use regular scoring and game format. B will "serve" next game.

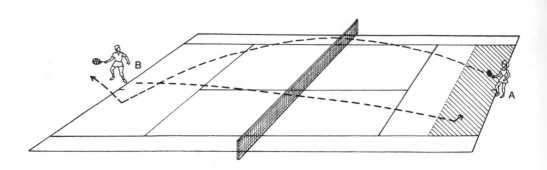

16. High on Groundstrokes

Emphasis: Groundstroke
Skill level: Intermediate, Advanced
Players/court: 2

Purpose: To develop the ability to return high-bouncing shots with the fore-hand and backhand.

Procedure: Both players stand at the baseline. A feeds a high-bouncing ball to B's forehand. B attempts to drive the ball deep into the court. Player A feeds the next high-bouncing ball to B's backhand and continues alternating fore-hands and backhands. After five minutes, players rotate.

17. Suicide

Emphasis: Groundstroke, Conditioning
Skill level: Intermediate, Advanced
Players/court: 3

Purpose: To develop a defensive crosscourt return with emphasis on a quick recovery.

Procedure: With all three players at the baseline, A feeds the ball crosscourt to C. C moves to return the ball crosscourt. As soon as C hits the ball, B feeds another ball crosscourt to C. C runs to the opposite corner to return the ball crosscourt. This pattern continues until C has returned ten good shots. Players then rotate.

18. Passing Shot

Emphasis: Groundstroke, Volley
Skill level: Intermediate, Advanced
Players/court: 2

Purpose: To develop a passing shot in a pressure situation.

Procedure: Player A at the net feeds a ball (to B's forehand) that lands in mid-backcourt. B returns the ball to A. Player A then volleys the ball, with pace, to B's backhand. B tries to pass A. Player A should start the drill to the side (forehand or backhand) in which B needs to build confidence. B's stronger side should receive the volley with greater pace. Gradually, B's weaker side should receive increased pressure. After ten minutes, players rotate.

NOTE—To hit with greater pace is to hit the ball with more speed.

Contributor—Richard Leach, Men's Tennis Coach, University of Southern California, Los Angeles, California.

19. Disguise

Emphasis: Groundstroke
Skill level: Advanced
Players/court: 2

Purpose: To develop the ability to disguise groundstrokes.

Procedure: Both players stand at the center of the baseline. Player A feeds a ball to B's forehand in the mid-backcourt. Just as B prepares to return the ball, A must guess whether the ball will be returned down-the-line or crosscourt and points in that direction. If the guess is incorrect, B gets the point. After eleven forehands have been returned, A feeds the same to B's backhand. After eleven backhands, players rotate.

Variations:
1. Instead of merely pointing to the area, A moves to either the right or the left. If A has guessed correctly the players can play out the point. B wins the point if A guesses incorrectly or commits an error. Player A gets one point for guessing correctly and a second point for winning a point that is played out.
2. A drop shot is added as a third possible return. Player A must guess right, left, or short.

Contributor—Alex Mayer, Centenary College, Mendham, New Jersey.

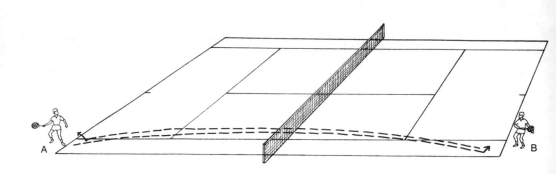

20. Alley Rally

Emphasis: Groundstroke
Skill level: Advanced
Players/court: 2 or 4

Purpose: To improve down-the-line placement.

Procedure: Players A and B stand at opposite ends of the alley, behind the baseline. Player A begins the rally by drop hitting the ball to B. The object is to keep the ball inside the alley, but the rally continues even if the ball goes out. Each time a player's return lands inside the alley that player earns a point. Players keep track of their opponent's score by calling out the total number of points whenever the ball lands inside. To allow each player to practice both forehand and backhand shots, A and B should switch positions after 5 minutes.

2 Midcourt Drills

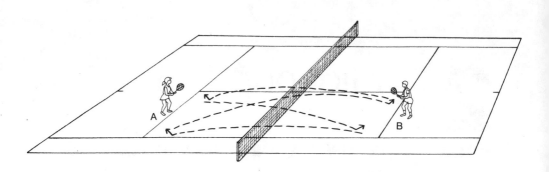

21. Midcourt Volley

Emphasis: Volley, Half Volley
Skill level: Intermediate, Advanced
Players/court: 2 or 4

Purpose: To develop placement of midcourt volley.

Procedure: Both players stand at midcourt. A hits crosscourt to B, alternating forehand and backhand strokes. B returns down-the-line, also alternating forehand and backhand strokes. After ten consecutive hits, B switches to crosscourt shots and A hits down-the-line.

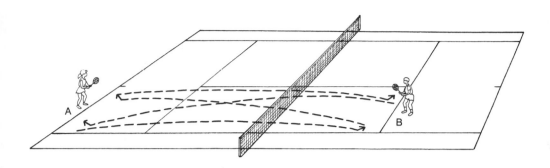

22. Backcourt To Midcourt

Emphasis: Volley, Half Volley, Groundstroke
Skill level: Intermediate, Advanced
Players/court: 2 or 4

Purpose: To develop control and placement with groundstrokes and volleys.

Procedure: Player A stands at baseline while B is at midcourt. Player A hits groundstrokes to B, alternating forehands and backhands. B returns with volleys, alternating forehands and backhands. After two minutes, or ten consecutive hits, players rotate positions.

Variation: Players follow the same procedure, hitting the ball crosscourt both ways.

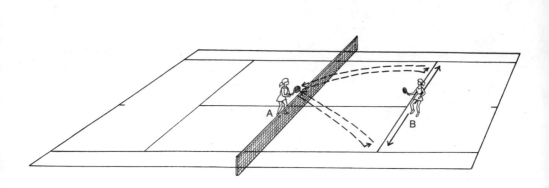

23. Side To Side

Emphasis: Half Volley, Volley, Conditioning
Skill level: Intermediate, Advanced
Players/court: 2

Purpose: To develop stamina, footwork, and balance while hitting from the midcourt.

Procedure: Player A at the net feeds a short ball wide to B's forehand. B, standing on the service line, runs to return the ball softly to A. Player A volleys a short ball wide to B's backhand. B, with toes on the service line, runs to return the ball softly to A. This pattern continues for three minutes. Player A should have an extra ball or two to feed in case of an error. After three minutes, players rotate.

24. Freeze Frame

Emphasis: Footwork, Conditioning, Approach
Skill level: Beginner, Intermediate, Advanced
Players/court: 2 or 4

Purpose: To develop footwork and controlled hitting from midcourt.

Procedure: Player A begins on the center mark at the baseline and B is at the net. B tosses the ball (underhand for more time to get to the ball, overhand for less time, adjusting to the skill level of the hitter) to land in the area marked (1). A moves to the ball, hits down-the-line, checks (freezes for an instant to check body balance and follow-through), and then side-steps back to center mark as fast as possible. As soon as A reaches the center mark, B tosses another ball. C and D do the same on the other half of the court. After three minutes, B and D move to the baseline while A and C become tossers. At the end of the second round, the four switch sides of the court so that all players hit both forehands and backhands.

Contributor—Cindy Young, Tennis Pro, Michigan City, Indiana.

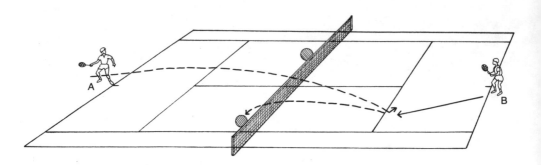

25. Drop It Over

Emphasis: Drop Shot
Skill level: Intermediate, Advanced
Players/court: 2

Purpose: To develop the touch of a drop shot.

Procedure: Both A and B are at the baseline. A feeds the ball to B's back-hand. The ball lands in midcourt and B moves in to return it with a drop shot aimed down-the-line to the target (shaded) area. A feeds another ball to B's backhand. B returns this one with a drop shot aimed crosscourt to the other target area. Player A feeds the next two balls to B's forehand. B returns them alternately down-the-line and crosscourt. After each shot, B returns to the baseline. After five minutes, players rotate.

26. Short Crosscourt

Emphasis: Groundstroke
Skill level: Advanced
Players/court: 2

Purpose: To practice hitting the short crosscourt shot.

Procedure: Players A and B start a crosscourt rally from the baseline. Whenever a ball lands in the midcourt, the player steps in and returns with a short crosscourt shot for a winner (a shot that cannot be returned). After five minutes of forehand practice, players switch to backhand.

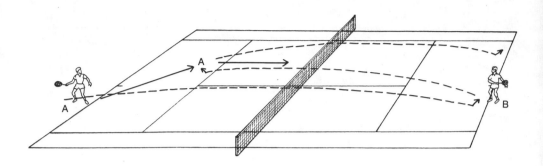

27. Go For It

Emphasis: Approach, Groundstroke, Volley
Skill level: Intermediate, Advanced
Players/court: 2

Purpose: To encourage players to take advantage of midcourt shots.

Procedure: Players A and B are at the baseline. They begin a rally attempting to keep the ball deep. By hitting deep, each player is attempting to draw a midcourt return from the other. When the midcourt ball comes, the player hits an approach shot and follows to the net to play out the point. The point begins with the short ball. Play eleven points.

28. Approach Shot To Target

Emphasis: Approach
Skill level: Intermediate, Advanced
Players/court: 2

Purpose: To develop a consistent, deep, down-the-line approach shot.

Procedure: Player A stands at the baseline while B is at midcourt. B feeds a short ball to A's forehand. Player A moves in and hits an approach shot down-the-line to the target (shaded area). The next ball is hit to A's backhand. This continues with alternate forehand and backhand shots. After five minutes, players rotate.

29. Three-Ball Approach And Volley

Emphasis: Approach, Volley
Skill level: Intermediate, Advanced
Players/court: 2 or 3

Purpose: To develop an approach shot followed by movement to the net.

Procedure: Player B takes the position at the middle of the baseline. Standing to one side of middle with three balls in hand, A feeds a ball down-the-line that lands in midcourt. B moves in to hit a down-the-line approach shot and follows the shot to the net. Player A feeds the second ball to B, who volleys deep and closes in on the net. Player A feeds the third ball to B, who puts it away with a volley. After five minutes, move to the other side of the court. After practicing both the forehand and backhand, players rotate.

Variations:
1. Player A can alternate forehand and backhand feeds with the second and third ball.
2. To encourage accuracy, B will not receive a second ball unless the first lands in the court, and B will not have a third ball unless the second one lands in the court.
3. C should be ready at the baseline as soon as B steps off the court.

30. Four-Ball Approach, Volley, And Overhead

Emphasis: Approach, Volley, Overhead
Skill level: Intermediate, Advanced
Players/court: 2

Purpose: To develop the ability to move up and back at the net with control.

Procedure: Players A and B start at the baseline. A feeds a ball down-the-line to B's backhand that lands in midcourt. B moves in to hit an approach shot deep down-the-line, and moves to the service line. Player A feeds the second ball to B's backhand. B volleys deep crosscourt and closes in on the net. A feeds the third ball to B's backhand. B hits a short, angled volley. A feeds a lob with the fourth ball that B returns deep to either corner with an overhead. After five minutes, A feeds all balls to B's forehand. After practicing the forehand, players rotate.

3 Volley Drills

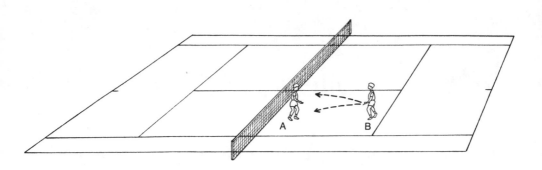

31. Toss-Catch Volley

Emphasis: Volley
Skill level: Beginner
Players/court: 2 or group

Purpose: To introduce proper body position for the volley.

Procedure: Players A and B stand approximately twelve feet apart. B tosses the ball underhand to A's forehand side. A steps across and forward with the left foot and reaches forward to catch the ball with the right hand. After ten tosses to the forehand side, B tosses ten to the backhand side. A steps across and forward with the right foot and reaches forward to catch the ball with the right hand. Players then rotate.

NOTE—Emphasis is on reaching forward and getting the arms away from the body. The partner should toss the ball a good distance away from the center of the hitter so that the hitter will have room to step across with the opposite foot.

32. Volley Shadow Drill

Emphasis: Volley
Skill level: Beginner
Players/court: 1 to Group

Purpose: To develop proper technique of forehand and backhand volley without the distraction of the ball and opponent.

Procedure: From the ready position, complete twenty forehand volleys. Take time to check the grip, footwork, contact zone, follow-through, and recovery to ready position. Practice high, low, close, and wide volleys. Follow same procedure to complete twenty backhand volleys. Then complete twenty volleys alternating forehand and backhand.

33. Volley Toss

Emphasis: Volley
Skill level: Beginner
Players/court: 2, 4, 6

Purpose: To introduce the volley.

Procedure: With both players at the net, A tosses the ball to B's forehand and B attempts to volley back to A. A catches the ball. After ten forehand volleys, A tosses ten to the backhand, then tosses ten more, alternating forehand and backhand. Players rotate.

Variation: After releasing the ball, the tosser moves to the right or left. The hitter must return the ball to the tosser.

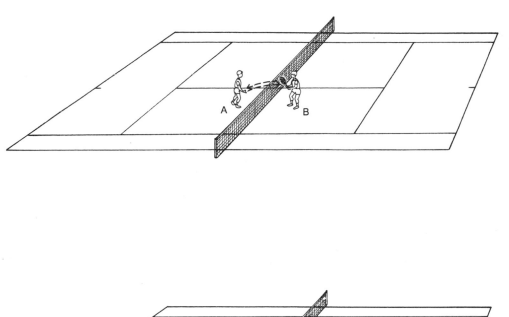

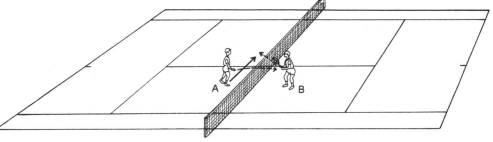

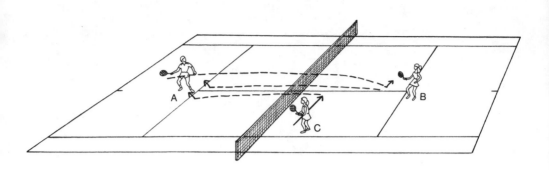

34. Intro to Poaching

Emphasis: Volley, Groundstroke
Skill level: Beginner, Intermediate
Players/court: 3

Purpose: To develop the sense of timing and lateral movement needed to poach.

Procedure: Players A and B stand at center just behind the service line and hit midcourt groundstrokes. C, at the net in the middle of the backhand service court, moves across to volley every other shot back to A. The players are attempting to keep one ball in play. C recovers to original position after each volley. After three minutes, C moves to the forehand service court to practice backhand volleys. After three minutes, players rotate.

Variation: Still hitting every other ball, C alternates forehand and backhand volleys, moving to opposite sides of the court after each volley.

35. Twenty-Five

Emphasis: Volley
Skill level: Beginner, Intermediate, Advanced
Players/court: 2 or 4

Purpose: To practice volleys in a competitive situation.

Procedure: Both players start at midservice court. Player A puts the ball into play. There must be three hits before the point actually begins—A's first hit, B's return, and A's return. The players must hit the ball within reach of each other throughout the point. If the ball is hit in bounds but out of reach, no one earns the point. B will start the next point and continue to alternate. The first player to reach twenty-five points wins the game.

36.   Angles, Angles, Angles, Angles

Emphasis: Volley
Skill level: Intermediate, Advanced
Players/court: 2

Purpose: To develop an awareness of and an ability to volley to the open court.

Procedure: In all four of the following variations, A feeds the ball from the baseline to B, who is at the net to volley. B stands a step away from the center service line, on the same side of the line as A, and closes in at the net to volley.

Variations:
1.   A stands at the backhand corner and feeds down-the-line to B's forehand.
2.   A stands at the backhand corner and feeds crosscourt to B's backhand.
3.   A stands at the forehand corner and feeds down-the-line to B's backhand.
4.   A stands at the forehand corner and feeds crosscourt to B's forehand.

1.

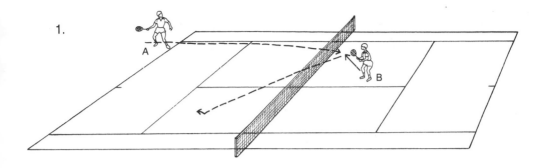

2.

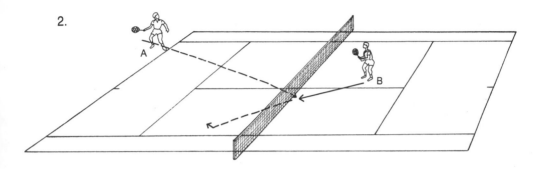

3.

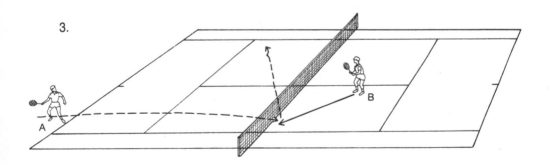

4.

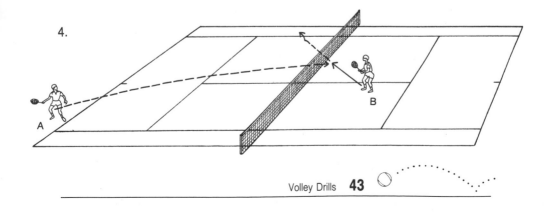

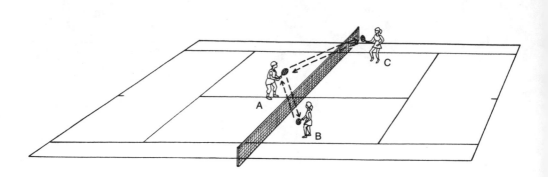

37. Three At Net

Emphasis: Volley, Half Volley
Skill level: Intermediate, Advanced
Players/court: 3

Purpose: To develop placement of volley and half volley.

Procedure: Three players are at the net. A is on the center service line, and B and C are closer to the singles sideline. A hits volleys to B and C alternately. B and C return the volleys to A. After three minutes players rotate so that all have equal time at the net. (However, if A is more skilled than B and C, A can remain the single player.)

Variation: Players stand on the service line to practice midcourt volley and half volley.

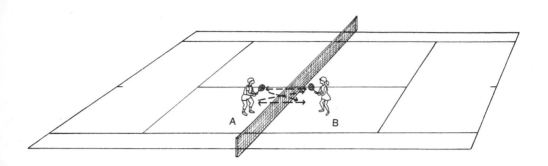

38. Forecourt Volley

Emphasis: Volley
Skill level: Intermediate, Advanced
Players/court: 2 or 4

Purpose: To develop placement of forecourt volley.

Procedure: Both players are at the net hitting ten consecutive shots for each of the following patterns:
1. Crosscourt forehands.
2. Crosscourt backhands.
3. Down-the-line forehand to backhand.
4. Down-the-line backhand to forehand.
5. Player A hits crosscourt, alternating forehand and backhand strokes, while B returns down-the-line, also alternating forehand and backhand.
6. Same as #5 above with B hitting crosscourt and A hitting down-the-line.

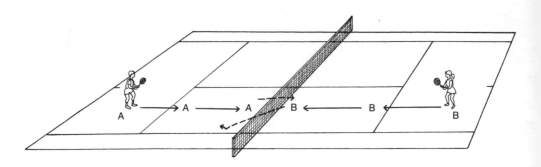

39. Closing In

Emphasis: Volley
Skill level: Intermediate, Advanced
Players/court: 2 or 4

Purpose: To develop the ability to volley while moving into the forecourt.

Procedure: Using only half the court, players start midway between the base-line and the service line. A drop hits the ball to B and moves in one step at a time using the split-step stop. B returns the ball and moves in one step at a time using the split-step stop. Both players attempt to keep the ball in play until arriving in the forecourt. When both players are in the forecourt, they try to win the point. Both play out fifteen points.

NOTE—Refer to drill 99, Split-Step Shadow Drill, for further explanation of the split-step stop.

40. King Of The Court

Emphasis: Volley, Groundstroke
Skill level: Intermediate, Advanced
Players/court: Group

Purpose: To develop the ability to react quickly at the net and to improve placement.

Procedure: Players use only half of the court (shaded area is out of bounds). Player A stands at the net. The rest of the group forms a line behind B, who stands just inside the baseline. A feeds a midcourt shot to B. B's first return should be directly back to A. After the first shot, B moves in to try to shoot past A. A and B play out the point. Then B moves to the end of the line and the next player steps in to play a point against A. The baseline player who wins two points from A becomes "King of the Court."

41. Getting To Know You

Emphasis: Volley, Groundstroke
Skill level: Intermediate, Advanced
Players/court: 3, 4, 6, 8

Purpose: To practice placement of volley and groundstrokes while providing movement at the net.

Procedure: Using one half of the court, Player C at the baseline hits a groundstroke between A and B at the net. Player A steps in to volley the first ball back to C. C returns the ball between A and B. B steps in to volley the second ball back to C. This pattern continues with A and B alternating hits. After a couple of minutes, A and B switch positions at the net so that each practices both forehand and backhand volleys. At this time, D can replace C to hit the groundstrokes. The three could rotate after five minutes or, if doubles partners want to stay together, C's partner could join C at the net while A and B move back to the baseline.

NOTE—It is important for the players at the net to step in to take the shot and recover to their position for the next ball.

Variations:
1. To create more movement for the net players, A and B stand on either side and within reach of the center service line and take alternate shots.
2. Instead of taking alternate shots, A and B can call for the shot, depending on who is in the best position.

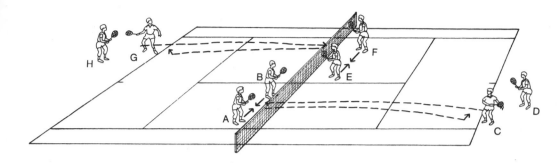

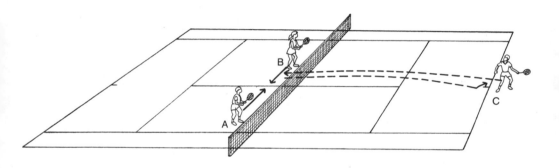

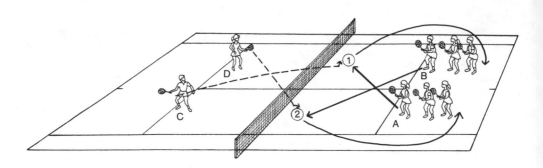

42. Cross-Over Volleys

Emphasis: Volley
Skill level: Intermediate, Advanced
Players/court: Group

Purpose: To develop body control on running volleys.

Procedure: Players form two rows behind the service line. Player A leads the row on the left-hand side of the court, B on the right. C and D stand across the net just inside the service line and act as feeders. C feeds crosscourt to Spot 1 in the forecourt. As the ball is hit, A must run to the spot and volley. As soon as that ball is hit, D feeds crosscourt to Spot 2 in the forecourt. As the ball is hit, B must run to the spot and volley. As soon as the players hit their volley, they return to the end of the opposite line. After two minutes, rotate feeders until everyone has had a chance to feed.

Variation: Stipulate either crosscourt or down-the-line volleys.

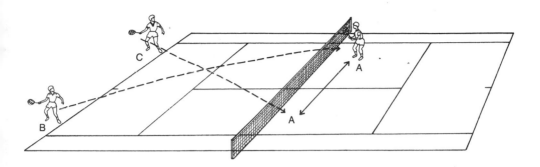

43. Two-On-One Volleys

Emphasis: Volley
Skill level: Intermediate, Advanced
Players/court: 3

Purpose: To practice the volley on the run.

Procedure: Player A is at the net while B and C are at the baseline. B feeds the ball crosscourt to A. A moves to hit short, angled volleys. As soon as A hits the ball, C feeds the next ball crosscourt to A. B and C continue feeding alternating crosscourt shots to A.

NOTE—Ideally, two feeders should be used in this drill to pressure the net player into a wider angle of lateral movement. However, the drill can be executed with a single feeder.

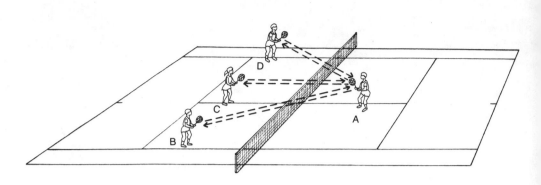

44. Yo-Yo

Emphasis: Volley
Skill level: Intermediate, Advanced
Players/court: 4

Purpose: To improve placement of volleys and to develop angled volleys.

Procedure: Player A stands at midservice court in the center of the court. B, C, and D stand at midservice court on the other side of the net. B is on one singles sideline, C is in the center, and D is on the other singles sideline. The four attempt to keep one ball in play for as long as possible. B, C, and D must always hit back to A. A must hit to B, C, and D in that order. After three minutes, players rotate to allow each player to have the single spot.

Variation: Player A hits only to B and D, keeping the ball away from C. If the ball is hit to C, C should put it away.

45. Volley At Wall

Emphasis: Volley
Skill level: Intermediate, Advanced
Players/court: 1

Purpose: To improve footwork and stroke needed for volley.

Procedure: With chalk or removable tape mark a three-foot target on a wall or backboard. The bottom edge should be five feet from the ground. Begin by standing approximately ten feet from the wall and hit consecutive volleys at the target. Keep a record of the number of your consecutive on-target shots and try to improve it.

Variations:
1. To practice hitting the ball on the move, advance to within three feet of the wall while keeping the ball in play.
2. Alternate forehand and backhand volleys.

46. Volley Dexterity

Emphasis: Volley
Skill level: Intermediate, Advanced
Players/court: Group

Purpose: To encourage players to be alert at the net and to develop quick hands.

Procedure: The group is evenly divided, with each player facing another across the net. The object is to volley the ball successfully from the first player to the last and back again. If there are eight players in the group, the ball should move in sequence from player 1 to player 8 and back again to 1. Each player has a spare ball in case a mistake occurs. Each time the ball completes a round trip, the players rotate one position clockwise and attempt the drill again.

Variations:
1. If there are two or more teams, a contest may be played to see which team completes the most round trips.
2. Once a mistake is made the player is eliminated, until there is a winner. The remaining players must then readjust their positions to fill the hole.

Contributor—Dennis Van der Meer, Van der Meer Tennis University, P.O. Box 5902, Hilton Head Island, South Carolina.

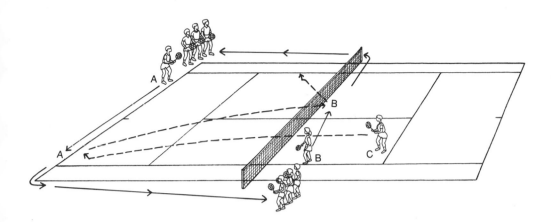

47. Crosscourt-Poach

Emphasis: Volley, Groundstroke, Doubles
Skill level: Intermediate, Advanced
Players/court: Group

Purpose: To develop groundstrokes and volleys moving laterally.

Procedure: Players form two lines, one headed by A at the baseline in the backhand corner, one headed by B at the net in the backhand service court. C, at midcourt, feeds a ball to A's forehand corner. A runs to return the shot crosscourt. B attempts to poach the return. Then A moves to the end of the line at the net, while B goes to the end of the line at the baseline. After six minutes in the backhand court, the players switch to the forehand court to practice backhand strokes.

Contributor—Cary Groth, Northern Illinois University, DeKalb, Illinois.

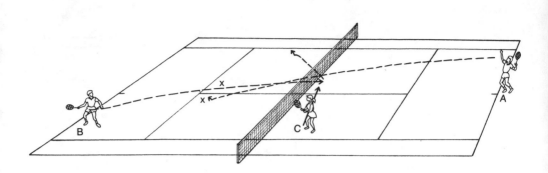

48. Poaching I

Emphasis: Volley, Serve, Service Return, Doubles
Skill level: Intermediate, Advanced
Players/court: 3

Purpose: To develop the ability to cut off a crosscourt service return in doubles.

Procedure: Player A attempts to serve all balls to the center (X) to cut down on the angle of B's return. B returns crosscourt. C moves across to volley the ball to the open court. Two balls are served to each court in turn (two to the forehand court, two to the backhand court). After B returns twelve balls, players rotate with A going to net, C to return service, and B to serve. After C returns twelve balls, players rotate again.

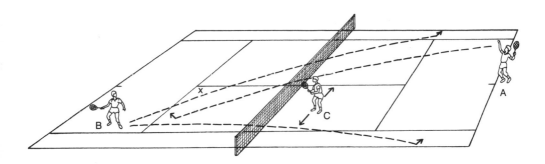

49. Poaching II

Emphasis: Volley, Serve, Service Return, Doubles
Skill level: Intermediate, Advanced
Players/court: 3

Purpose: To develop the net player's awareness of serve placement in relation to service returns and to develop an awareness of the net player's position by the player returning the serve.

Procedure: Player A serves to B, both to the backhand and forehand. C is ready to poach if the serve is down the center (X). B returns either crosscourt or down-the-line trying to pass C. Player A serves two balls to each court alternately. After B returns twelve balls, players rotate with A going to the net, C returning service, and B serving. After C returns twelve balls, players rotate again.

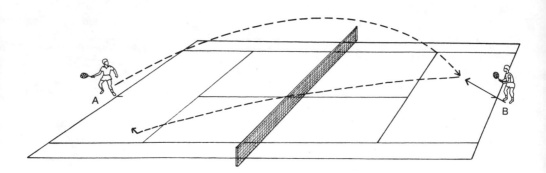

50. Volley The Moonball

Emphasis: Volley
Skill level: Intermediate, Advanced
Players/court: 2

Purpose: To develop the ability to volley in the backcourt and to avoid getting pinned against the fence.

Procedure: Players A and B are at the baseline. Player A feeds a high lob that will land at the baseline. B steps in before the bounce and hits a volley. A feeds alternate forehands and backhands. When twenty balls have been hit, players rotate.

51. Off To The Races

Emphasis: Volley
Skill level: Intermediate, Advanced
Players/court: 2

Purpose: To develop placement of drop volley.

Procedure: Player A feeds a ball from the baseline to B at the net. B attempts to drop volley to the target (shaded area). A good drop volley should pass low over the net and land close to it. A feeds alternate forehands and backhands to B. B returns alternately to Targets 1 and 2. After four minutes, players rotate.

4 Serve And Service Return Drills

52. Consecutive Serves

Emphasis: Serve
Skill level: Beginner, Intermediate, Advanced
Players/court: 1 to 4

Purpose: To practice concentration when serving.

Procedure: Player A serves to B, two serves to each court, alternating courts. When A misses, B serves. Keep track of the number of consecutive good serves by each player. Try to improve by increasing the number. Keep personal and group records to add an element of competition.

53. Jacks

Emphasis: Serve
Skill level: Beginner, Intermediate, Advanced
Players/court: 2 or 4

Purpose: To develop concentration and consistency in serving.

Procedure: Spin the racket to determine which player serves first. Player A serves one serve from the forehand court. If the serve is good, A moves to the backhand court to attempt two consecutive serves. If both are good, A attempts three consecutive serves from the forehand court. A continues serving until missing, alternating service courts and attempting an additional serve each time. If A misses, B serves. B follows the same pattern. If B misses, A serves. Player A will continue from the last successful set. (If the last set completed was three consecutive serves, then four consecutive serves should be attempted.) The object is to be the first player to serve ten consecutive successful serves.

54. Serve For Depth

Emphasis: Serve
Skill level: Beginner, Intermediate, Advanced
Players/court: 2 to 4

Purpose: To develop a deep serve.

Procedure: The service court is divided into four equal parts with lines parallel to the net and service line. Each part is given a point value from one to four (one point closest to the net, four at the service line). Player A serves two balls to each court alternately until twelve balls have been served. A receives the number of points corresponding to the area in which the ball lands. B then serves twelve balls. The player having the most points wins.

55. Target Serve

Emphasis: Serve
Skill level: Intermediate, Advanced
Players/court: 2 to 4

Purpose: To develop accuracy in serving.

Procedure: Mark a line three feet inside and parallel to the service line. Divide that area in half with another line. Make a pyramid with four balls in the center of each area to use as targets. Player A will serve two balls to the forehand court, the first to land in the forehand target area (1), the second to land in the backhand target area (2). A will then serve two balls to the backhand court, the first to land in the forehand target area (1), the second to land in the backhand target area (2). A will continue this pattern until twelve balls have been served, then B will serve twelve balls. Five points are awarded if the pyramid of balls is hit, three points if the serve lands in the proper target area, and one point if the serve lands anywhere in the correct service court but not in the proper target area. The player having the most points wins.

Variation: The target areas and five-point targets can vary in size, depending on the skill level of the players.

56. Only One

Emphasis: Serve, Singles, Doubles
Skill level: Beginner, Intermediate, Advanced
Players/court: 2 or 4

Purpose: To develop a consistent second serve.

Procedure: Play points or games with only one serve per point. The player or doubles team loses the point if the serve is out.

57. Serve and Volley Half-Court

Emphasis: Serve, Volley, Half Volley
Skill level: Intermediate, Advanced
Players/court: 2 or 4

Purpose: To practice following the serve to the net and to develop an offensive game.

Procedure: Using only half of the whole court (the shaded area is out of bounds), A serves down-the-line to B and follows the serve to the net. A and B play out the point. A serves ten points, then B serves ten points.

NOTE—B is not restricted to the baseline.

58. Doubles Serve and Volley

Emphasis: Serve, Service Return, Volley, Doubles
Skill level: Intermediate, Advanced
Players/court: 2

Purpose: To practice closing in on the net following both the serve and the service return in doubles.

Procedure: Player A serves from the doubles position in the forehand court and moves to the net. B returns the serve crosscourt to A and the point is played out crosscourt with both players closing in on the net. When playing in the forehand court, the backhand court is out of bounds (shaded area) and vice versa. The next point is served from the backhand court. Players rotate after ten points.

59. Serve-Return-Volley Pattern

Emphasis: Serve, Service Return, Volley
Skill level: Intermediate, Advanced
Players/court: 2

Purpose: To practice the serve, return, and volley in a controlled sequence.

Procedure: Player A serves from the forehand court and follows the serve to the net. B attempts to pass A down-the-line. A moves to the ball and volleys to the open court. A serves next from the backhand court. Again B attempts to pass A down-the-line. A moves to the ball and volleys to the open court. A continues alternating courts. With the next two points, B will try to pass crosscourt. After sixteen points are played, players rotate.

NOTE—The players are working together to get the three shots (serve, return, and volley). The server controls the serve so that the return can be hit to the proper area.

Variation: Instead of stopping after the three hits, let play continue until the point is over. Keep in mind that the first three shots are controlled. Make an attempt to move the other player around the court.

60. Lob Service Return

Emphasis: Service Return, Serve, Lob, Doubles
Skill level: Intermediate, Advanced
Players/court: 2

Purpose: To develop a lob return of service for doubles.

Procedure: Player A serves to B. B returns the serve down-the-line with a lob to land in the shaded area. This shot is intended to go over the head of the server's partner at the net and to catch the server rushing the net. A serves two balls to each court alternately. When B has returned twenty balls, players rotate.

61. Offensive Service Return

Emphasis: Service Return, Serve
Skill level: Intermediate, Advanced
Players/court: 2

Purpose: To develop the ability to step in and attack a weak or second serve.

Procedure: Player A serves a second serve to B. B attempts to step in closer and drive the ball to a specific target area. A serves two balls to each court alternately. After sixteen balls have been returned, players rotate.

Variations:
1. Target areas can be deep crosscourt and down-the-line.
2. Target areas can be short crosscourt and down-the-line.
3. B follows the service return to the net.

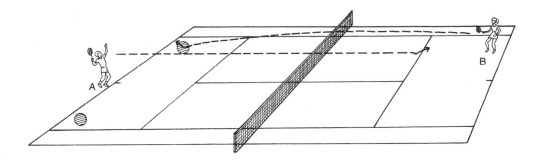

62. Serve and Deep Return

Emphasis: Service Return, Serve
Skill level: Intermediate, Advanced
Players/court: 2

Purpose: To develop placement on service return that is used when the server remains at the baseline.

Procedure: Player A serves two good serves to each court alternately. In returning the serves, B attempts to hit the target (shaded) areas. The first four returns (two from each court) are sent down-the-line, the next four to the cross-court target areas. Players repeat this pattern until B has returned sixteen balls, then rotate.

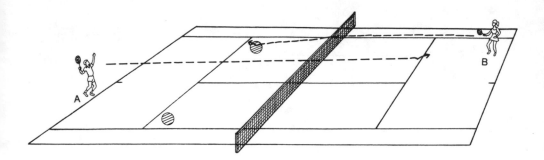

63. Serve and Short Return

Emphasis: Service Return, Serve
Skill level: Intermediate, Advanced
Players/court: 2

Purpose: To develop placement on service return that is needed when the server rushes the net.

Procedure: Player A serves two good serves to each court alternately. In returning the serves, B attempts to hit the target (shaded) areas. The first four returns (two from each court) are sent down-the-line, the next four to the cross-court target areas. Players repeat this pattern until B has returned sixteen balls, then rotate.

64. Crosscourt Alley Returns

Emphasis: Service Return, Serve, Doubles
Skill level: Intermediate, Advanced
Players/court: 2 or 4

Purpose: To develop a crosscourt service return in doubles.

Procedure: Player A serves to B. B returns the serve to the crosscourt alley. A serves two balls to each court alternately. When B has returned sixteen balls, players rotate.

Variation: If court space is limited, four players can use the same court, alternating sides.

65. Down-The-Line Alley Returns

Emphasis: Service Return, Serve, Doubles
Skill level: Intermediate, Advanced
Players/court: 2

Purpose: To develop a down-the-line service return in doubles.

Procedure: Player A serves to B. B returns the serve to the alley down-the-line. A serves two balls to each court alternately. When B has returned sixteen balls, players rotate.

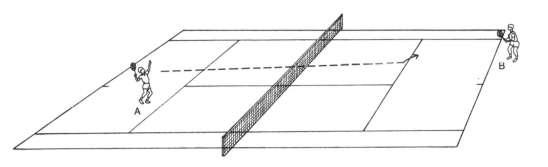

66. Quick Serve

Emphasis: Serve, Service Return
Skill level: Intermediate, Advanced
Players/court: 2

Purpose: To develop quicker reactions for the service return while providing a warm-up for the server.

Procedure: Player A stands midway between the baseline and service line to the right of center and serves to B. B then returns the serve. Player A serves two good serves to each court alternately. After B has returned sixteen balls, players rotate.

NOTE—This drill can be used to give the player an opportunity to practice returning a fast serve when the practice partner is not able to execute a consistent fast serve.

5 Lob And Overhead Drills

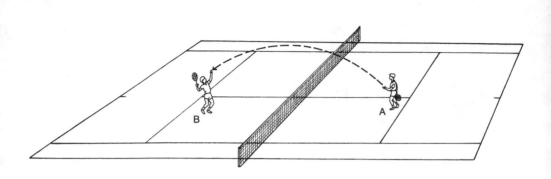

67. In Left Field

Emphasis: Overhead
Skill level: Beginner, Intermediate
Players/court: 2, 4, or 6

Purpose: To develop the ability to judge the flight of the ball when it is lobbed and to practice getting in position to hit the overhead.

Procedure: Players A and B stand just inside the service line. A tosses a high lob to B. B brings the racket back as if to hit an overhead, and reaches up to catch the ball with the free hand. The body should be in a position such that if the ball were not caught it would land on the player's forehead. B then tosses the ball in the same manner to A. A also catches it with the free hand.

Variation: As the ability to judge ball flight improves, player A can hit, instead of toss, the ball to B.

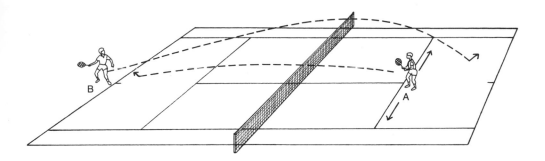

68. Deep Lobs

Emphasis: Lob
Skill level: Intermediate, Advanced
Players/court: 2

Purpose: To practice hitting deep lobs.

Procedure: Player A stands at the service line and feeds balls to B at the baseline. B attempts to lob the ball over A. A may move laterally, but not backwards. If A hits the ball, or if it goes out of bounds, A wins the point. If the lob goes over A and lands within bounds, B wins the point. Players should rotate after fifteen points.

Variation: As the players gain proficiency, the feeder is moved back another foot or two.

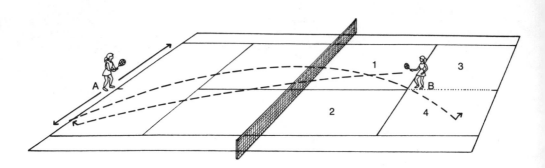

69. Lob To A Spot

Emphasis: Lob
Skill level: Intermediate, Advanced
Players/court: 2

Purpose: To develop a deep defensive lob.

Procedure: Player B at midcourt feeds the ball to A's forehand corner. Starting at the middle of the baseline, A runs to the ball and returns with a lob, attempting to hit the deep backhand area. B feeds the second ball to A's backhand corner. A runs to the ball and again tries to return it deep and to the backhand. B is feeding fast enough to keep A moving (but not sprinting) from forehand to backhand corners. However, B is always providing a challenge to A. Each quarter of the court is given a numerical value. A receives the point value of the area in which the lob lands. After ten balls are hit, players rotate. The player with the greater number of points wins.

70. Overhead Recovery

Emphasis: Overhead, Conditioning
Skill level: Intermediate, Advanced
Players/court: 2

Purpose: To practice hitting overheads when the ball is behind the player and recovering to a volley position after the hit.

Procedure: Player A stands at mid-service court. B, at the baseline, feeds lobs that will take A out of the service court. After returning the shot overhead, A must run and touch the net with the racket and get ready for the next shot. As soon as A touches the net, B feeds the next ball. Players rotate after three minutes.

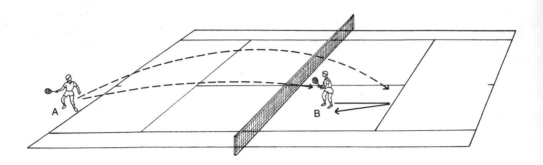

71. Volley-Overhead

Emphasis: Lob, Overhead, Volley
Skill level: Intermediate, Advanced
Players/court: 2 or 4

Purpose: To develop control with the overhead and volley and to practice closing in on the net after the overhead.

Procedure: Using half of the court, A is at the baseline and B starts in the middle of the service court. Player A hits drives and lobs alternately. A drives and B moves in for the volley. A then lobs and B moves back for the overhead. This pattern continues with each player trying to keep the ball in play. Players rotate after three minutes.

Variations:
1. Occasionally A hits a deep lob to the baseline.
2. So that players learn to read the impending lob, vary the sequence of the drill.

Contributor—Rosemary Fri, University of Northern Colorado, Greeley, Colorado.

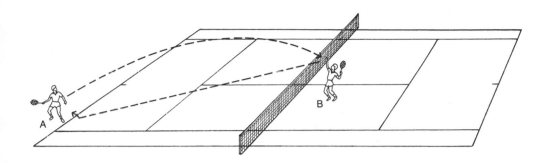

72. Lob-Overhead Rally

Emphasis: Lob, Overhead
Skill level: Intermediate, Advanced
Players/court: 2

Purpose: To develop control and placement of the lob and overhead.

Procedure: Player A in the forehand corner at the baseline feeds a lob to B standing at the net. B returns with an overhead. Both players attempt to keep the ball in play with lobs and overheads. After twenty balls are returned to the forehand corner, A moves to the backhand corner and continues the rally. When B has hit twenty balls to the backhand corner, players rotate.

73. Smash To Open Court

Emphasis: Overhead
Skill level: Intermediate, Advanced
Players/court: 2

Purpose: To develop an awareness of the open court.

Procedure: Player A at the baseline in the backhand corner feeds lobs to B at midcourt. B hits the overhead to the open forehand court. After ten balls have been hit, A moves to the forehand corner to feed ten balls. B hits to the open backhand court. After B has hit ten balls to each corner players rotate.

NOTE—The feeder should force the net player to move by feeding to the forehand, backhand, short and deep areas.

Variation: After feeding the ball to B from the backhand corner, A moves to the forehand corner leaving the backhand open. B hits to the open backhand court. The next ball is fed from the forehand corner. After feeding the ball, A runs to the backhand corner, and B returns to the open forehand court. After B returns twenty balls, players rotate.

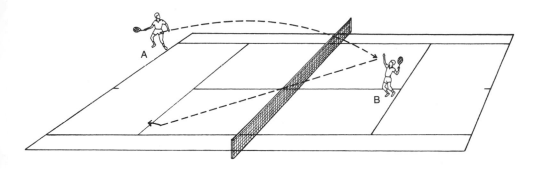

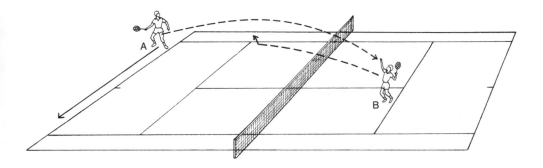

74. Angle Overheads

Emphasis: Overhead
Skill level: Intermediate, Advanced
Players/court: 2

Purpose: To develop control and placement with the overhead.

Procedure: Player A at the baseline feeds lobs to B at the net. B returns with overheads, attempting to hit in the shaded areas. After each overhead, B must touch the net with the racket to assure returning to the net position. A should wait until B has touched the net before feeding the next ball. After fifteen balls are hit in the target area, players rotate.

NOTE—The feeder should force the net player to move by feeding to the forehand, backhand, short, and deep areas.

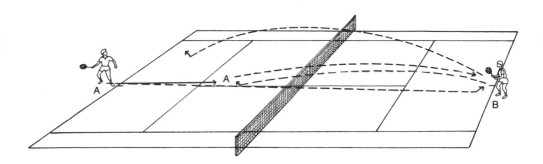

75. Lob and Pass

Emphasis: Lob, Overhead, Volley, Half Volley
Skill level: Intermediate, Advanced
Players/court: 2

Purpose: To improve baseline player's awareness of net player's position and to emphasize recovery to the net after hitting the overhead.

Procedure: Both players begin at the baseline. Player A puts the ball in play with a drop hit to B and moves to the net. There must be four hits before the point begins: A's drop hit, B's return, A's volley, and B's lob. The point is then played out with B alternating passing shots and lobs. Change roles after every point.

Variation: After the initial volley and overhead, Player B hits either passing shots or lobs, depending on Player A's position. (If player A does not recover to net position, B tries to pass. If Player A does recover to net, B lobs.)

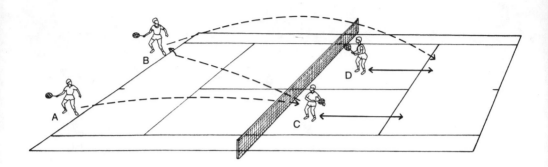

76. Two Up—Two Back

Emphasis: Lob, Overhead, Doubles
Skill level: Intermediate, Advanced
Players/court: 4

Purpose: To develop the overhead and lob for doubles and to practice teamwork.

Procedure: Player A or B at the baseline feeds a groundstroke to C or D at the net. C or D volleys the ball deep into the backcourt. A or B then tries to lob over C and D to get them away from the net. After returning the lob, C and D try to regain their net positions. A and B remain at the baseline and lob. After ten points are played, players rotate: C and D go to the baseline and A and B go to the net.

6

Drills For Singles And Doubles Play

77. Handicap Tennis

Emphasis: Singles, Doubles
Skill level: Beginner, Intermediate, Advanced
Players/court: 2 or 4

Purpose: To provide a challenge for both players when one is much more skilled than the other.

Procedure: The weaker player starts the game with a given number of points according to the difference in skill. The greater the difference, the more points the weaker player receives.

NOTE—The stronger player realizes it would not take much concentration or effort to beat the opponent until the opponent starts with a 30-love score.

Variation: In doubles, the weaker team is given the point advantage.

78. Tie Breakers

Emphasis: Singles, Doubles
Skill level: Beginner, Intermediate, Advanced
Players/court: 2

Purpose: To become familiar with the format of the 12-point tie breaker in singles and doubles.

Procedure: (Singles) Player A, having served the first game of the set, serves the first point from the right service court; B serves points 2 and 3 (left then right); A serves points 4 and 5 (left then right); B serves point 6 (left) and after they change ends of court, point 7 (right); A serves points 8 and 9 (left then right); B serves points 10 and 11 (left then right); and A serves point 12 (left). The player who reaches 7 points during these first 12 points wins the tie breaker. If the score has reached 6 points all, the players change ends and continue in the same pattern until one player establishes a margin of 2 points. Note that the players change ends every 6 points, and that the player who serves the last point of one of these 6-point segments also serves the first point of the next one (from the right service court).

Doubles follows the same pattern, with partners preserving their serving sequence. Players A and B are playing against C and D. Player A serves the first point (right); C serves points 2 and 3 (left then right); B serves points 4 and 5 (left then right); D serves point 6 (left) and the teams change ends. D serves point 7 (right); A serves points 8 and 9 (left then right); C serves points 10 and 11 (left then right); B serves point 12 (left). The team that wins 7 points during these first 12 points wins the tie breaker. If the score has reached 6 points all, the teams change ends. B then serves point 13 (right), and they continue until one team establishes a margin of 2 points and thus wins the tie breaker.

NOTE—In order to become more comfortable with the rules of the game, practice tie breakers in addition to playing sets. This is also an excellent way to play points when limited practice time prohibits a full set.

Variation: Play the best two of three tie breakers.

79. Earn-A-Serve

Emphasis: Singles
Skill level: Beginner, Intermediate, Advanced
Players/court: 2

Purpose: To encourage players to concentrate on each point.

Procedure: Players spin to determine who will serve. The point is played in a normal fashion. The player winning the point serves the next point. If the serving player wins four consecutive points, that player has won a game. When a game is completed, the serve goes to the other player. The goal is to win the most games.

80. Twenty-One

Emphasis: Singles, Groundstroke
Skill level: Intermediate, Advanced
Players/court: 2

Purpose: To practice groundstrokes competitively.

Procedure: Players start at the baseline. A puts the ball into play with a drop hit. There must be three hits before the point actually begins: A's drop hit, B's return, and A's return. Both players then play out the point. B will start the next point with a drop hit and players continue to alternate. The first player to reach twenty-one points wins the game.

NOTE—The first three hits are hit down the center. If any of the three are not returned, there is no loss of points. The point starts with the fourth hit.

81. Errors Can Be Costly

Emphasis: Singles
Skill level: Intermediate, Advanced
Players/court: 2

Purpose: To improve concentration and steadiness.

Procedure: Players begin at the baseline. A puts the ball into play with a drop hit to B. There must be three hits before the point begins: A's drop hit, B's return, and A's return. The point is then played out as in a singles game. If either player makes a forced error, no point is scored. If either player makes an unforced error, the opponent earns one point. If either player hits a winner, that player earns one point. The first player to earn ten points is the winner.

NOTE—A forced error is made when a player fails to return a well-hit shot. An unforced error is made when a player fails to return an easy shot. A winner is a shot that the opponent cannot reach.

Contributor—Karen Grummell, Tennis Pro, South Bend, Indiana.

82. Thirty-One

Emphasis: Singles
Skill level: Intermediate, Advanced
Players/court: 2

Purpose: To encourage deep groundstrokes and aggressive play.

Procedure: Both players begin at the baseline. A puts the ball into play with a drop hit to B. There must be three hits before the point begins: A's drop hit, B's return, and A's return. The point is then played out as in a singles game. If B hits the ball out of bounds, A wins one point. If B hits the ball into the net, A wins two points. If B hits a winner (a ball that A cannot reach) B wins three points, and vice versa. The first player to earn thirty-one points wins the game.

83. Up Together

Emphasis: Doubles
Skill level: Intermediate, Advanced
Players/court: 4

Purpose: To practice moving to the net together and to develop communication between doubles partners.

Procedure: Players A, B, C, and D start a rally from the baseline. When a ball lands in the forecourt or midcourt, the team takes the opportunity to move to the net. To assure good communication and teamwork, the player returning the short ball (in this case, B) says, "Let's go," and both players move to the net. The point is played out. C and D also look for an opportunity to move in to the net with the first short ball hit to them.

NOTE—Gaining the net position is essential in good doubles. Playing in the backcourt is generally defensive and temporary. However, the transition from backcourt to forecourt requires good communication and practice. As a general rule, when players are in the backcourt looking for an opportunity to take the net, they move in on a ball landing in the forecourt or midcourt. However, the player returning the ball is the best judge of whether it is a strong return that should be followed to the net or a weak return that may require the players to remain in the backcourt.

84. Keep Them Away

Emphasis: Doubles, Lob, Overhead, Groundstroke, Volley
Skill level: Intermediate, Advanced
Players/court: 4

Purpose: To practice keeping the opposing doubles team away from the net and to develop teamwork.

Procedure: Two teams rally from the baseline. When a ball lands in their midcourt, that team will attempt to return the shot and move in together to the net. Their opponents then attempt to get them away from the net with a deep lob. For example, after returning a midcourt shot, C and D move to the net. A or B attempts a deep lob. If the lob is successful, A and B close in on the net together. If the lob is short and C or D returns with an overhead, C and D continue to move in on the net. If A and B should gain the net position, C or D attempts a deep lob to drive them back.

NOTE—If a team does not close in on the net, but stays in midcourt expecting the lob, the other team should try to pass them.

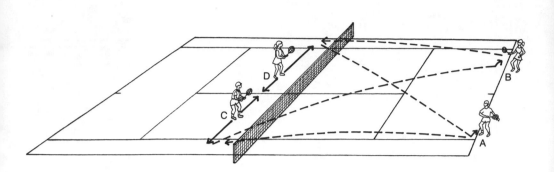

85. Siamese Twins

Emphasis: Doubles, Groundstroke, Volley
Skill level: Intermediate, Advanced
Players/court: 4

Purpose: To develop the ability to move together laterally in relation to the ball.

Procedure: Players A and B are at the baseline and C and D are at the net. Player A feeds down-the-line to C. As C moves to return the ball crosscourt to B, D moves to cover the middle. B returns down-the-line to D. As D moves to return the ball crosscourt to A, C moves to cover the middle. If A or B cannot keep the ball in play, they should have an extra ball in hand to keep the pattern of lateral movement going. After three minutes, A and B hit crosscourt, and C and D hit down-the-line. After three more minutes, the teams rotate.

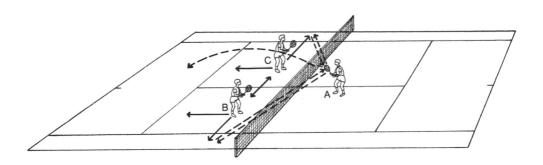

86. Team Work

Emphasis: Doubles, Volley
Skill level: Intermediate, Advanced
Players/court: 3

Purpose: To practice parallel positioning in doubles.

Procedure: Player A is at the net, gently hitting balls to B and C, aiming randomly to either side or between them. B and C are doubles partners and must move together. When the ball is hit to one side, both B and C must move to that side, maintaining the distance between them so that the middle is covered by one or the other. When a shot is hit between them, B or C must call for it, gently returning the ball to A. Occasionally, A should hit a deep lob so that B and C can practice moving backwards together. After returning the lob, B and C should return together to the net. After two minutes of continuous movement, players should rotate positions.

NOTE—Generally the player with the stronger stroke (most often the forehand) takes the ball down the middle. The partners may want to decide who should take the middle shot before they take the court.

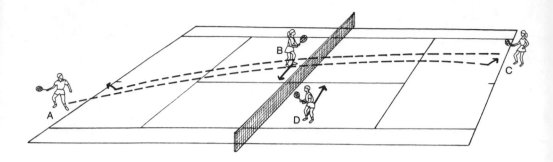

87. Keep Away

Emphasis: Doubles, Groundstroke, Volley
Skill level: Intermediate, Advanced
Players/court: 4

Purpose: To develop a crosscourt shot and a poach shot in doubles.

Procedure: Players A and C in the backcourt play against B and D at the net. A and C attempt to keep a crosscourt rally going, while B and D attempt to poach. After four minutes, players rotate one position clockwise, with A and C at the net and B and D in the backcourt. The next rotation finds A and C in the backcourt hitting backhand crosscourt, and B and D at the net hitting backhand volleys. After another four minutes, A and C will be at the net, B and D in the backcourt. The backcourt players keep count of consecutive hits. The team with the greater number at the end of the drill wins.

7 Footwork and Conditioning Drills

88. Cover Drill

Emphasis: Conditioning
Skill level: Beginner, Intermediate, Advanced
Players/court: 1 to Group

Purpose: To strengthen arm muscles while practicing swing.

Procedure: Put the racket cover on the racket and take practice swings—low and high forehands, low and high backhands, and serves. As the arm gets stronger, put a tennis ball inside the cover. Continue adding one ball at a time as arm strength increases.

89. Air Dribble

Emphasis: Conditioning
Skill level: Beginner
Players/court: 1 to group

Purpose: To develop an awareness of the "sweet spot" and to develop wrist and arm strength.

Procedure: Using the forehand grip, continuously bounce the ball up in the air without allowing it to hit the ground. Attempt twenty consecutive hits using the forehand side of the racket. Then try twenty consecutive hits using the backhand side of the racket. Finally, attempt to alternate each bounce with the forehand and backhand side of the racket.

90. Book Work

Emphasis: Conditioning
Skill level: Beginner, Intermediate, Advanced
Players/court: 1 to group

Purpose: To develop strength in wrist, forearm, calves, and ankles.

Procedure:
1. Hold a heavy book in your outstretched hand with your palm facing down. Without moving the arm, lift the book up as far as it will go and then lower it. Repeat this ten times.
2. Turn your arm so that your palm is facing up. Continue to raise and lower the book. Repeat this ten times.
3. Do the same with the other hand. As strength develops, increase the number of repetitions.
4. While raising and lowering the book, move up and down on your toes to increase strength in the calves and ankles.

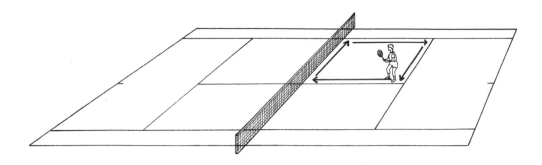

91. Four Direction Footwork

Emphasis: Footwork, Conditioning
Skill level: Beginner, Intermediate, Advanced
Players/court: 1 to 4

Purpose: To improve footwork and agility.

Procedure: The player starts at the service line in the center of the court. Always facing the net, the player runs forward to the net, slides to the right to the singles line, runs backward to the service line, and then slides to the left to the center service line. Repeat ten times, rest for one minute, repeat ten times.

Contributor—Jan Helfrich, Central Michigan University, Mt. Pleasant, Michigan.

92. Pick 'Em Up, Put 'Em Down

Emphasis: Conditioning
Skill level: Beginner, Intermediate, Advanced
Players/court: 1 to 8

Purpose: To improve footwork, agility, and leg strength.

Procedure: The player has four balls on a racket next to the court. The player takes the first ball, runs to the far doubles side line and places the ball on the line. The player then runs back to get the second ball and places it on the far singles line. The third ball is placed on the center service line, the fourth on the near singles side line. As soon as the last ball is down, the player repeats the pattern picking up the balls and returning them to the racket. This is a timed drill. Players are encouraged to stay low to enhance quickness.

Variations: The direction of the run can be varied:
1. Running forward in both directions.
2. Running forward in one direction and backwards in the other direction.
3. Moving laterally with a shuffle and always facing the net in both directions.
4. Carioca step facing the net.

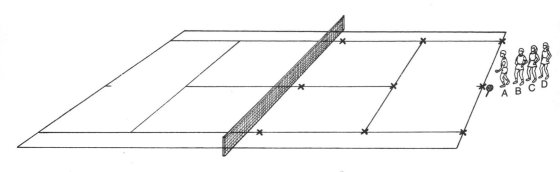

93. Nine-Ball Pick Up

Emphasis: Conditioning
Skill level: Beginner, Intermediate, Advanced
Players/court: Group

Purpose: To develop quickness and agility.

Procedure: Place nine balls on the strings of a racket and lay the racket on the ground behind the baseline at the center of the court. Taking only one ball at a time, Player A distributes them around the court at various designated locations (X). B then picks them up, also one at a time, and returns them to the racket. The pattern of alternately placing and retrieving the nine balls continues until all members of the group have participated. This drill can be played as a relay race, with half of the group competing against the other half.

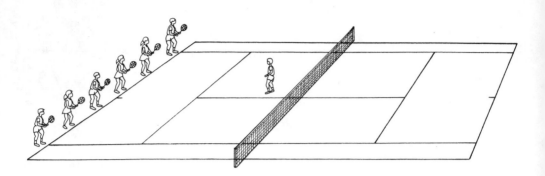

94. Hit It

Emphasis: Conditioning
Skill level: Beginner, Intermediate, Advanced
Players/court: Group

Purpose: To develop footwork, quickness, and stamina.

Procedure: The players spread out along the baseline. The leader stands at the net facing the group. The leader gives the following verbal cues at random, and the players respond as quickly as possible:
- Hit it: players move their feet rapidly in place.
- Left: players, facing the net, shuffle to their left.
- Right: players, facing the net, shuffle to their right.
- Up: players run to touch the net and run back for an overhead.
- Split: players take a split step to stop.
- Back: players run back for an overhead.

The leader needs to change direction commands quickly. After players get back to the baseline, they rest for fifteen seconds. This is repeated six times.

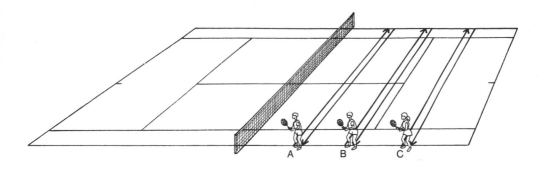

95. Jack Rabbit

Emphasis: Footwork, Conditioning
Skill level: Beginner, Intermediate, Advanced
Players/court: 1 to 8

Purpose: To improve stamina, agility, and quickness.

Procedure: Players start at one doubles sideline and sprint to the other doubles sideline and back. They must touch the line with one hand. While running, players face the net, trying to keep their shoulders square to the net. Sprint the pattern for thirty seconds and then rest for thirty seconds. Repeat twice.

Variations:
1. Players sprint holding a racket and touch the line with the racket.
2. Players sprint holding a racket and swing at an imaginary ball when arriving at each alley, forehand at one alley and backhand at the other. They should not pause after swinging but allow the follow-through of the swing to take them to the other side.

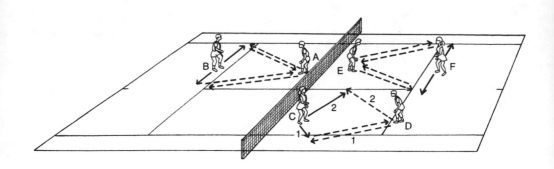

96. Ball Roll

Emphasis: Conditioning, Footwork
Skill level: Beginner, Intermediate, Advanced
Players/court: 2, 4, 6, 8

Purpose: To develop agility and stamina.

Procedure: Player A needs three balls (two to roll and one extra). Player A rolls the first ball to the corner of the service court. B shuffles along the service line to retrieve the ball. Player B rolls the ball back to A. As soon as B has let go of the first ball, A rolls the second ball to the opposite corner of the service court. B runs to retrieve the second ball and returns it to A. This pattern continues for thirty seconds, then players rotate.

Variations:
1. Change direction on the runner. Occasionally, roll the ball behind the runner. As the runner turns to sprint to the opposite corner, roll the ball to the same corner the runner just left.
2. In addition to providing lateral movement, roll some balls short to make the runner run forward and then move back for the next ball (C and D).
3. As players improve cardiovascular and muscular endurance, increase the length of time for the drill.

NOTE—The player rolling the ball should aim at the corners so that the runner covers a good distance before turning to run in the other direction. The running player needs to bend at the knees to develop the leg muscles necessary for changing directions quickly. When using four players on the same side of the court, switch the position of the roller and the runner to avoid collisions.

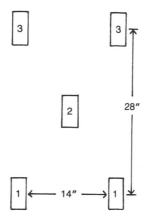

97. Hopscotch

Emphasis: Footwork
Skill level: Beginner, Intermediate, Advanced
Players/court: 1 to Group

Purpose: To develop foot mobility and balance.

Procedure: Following the diagram, mark five boxes on the floor or ground with tape or chalk. Begin with both feet on parallel boxes (1). Hop on left foot to middle box (2), and then onto both feet to parallel boxes (3). Making a 180° turn in the air to the left, land with both feet on parallel boxes (3) again. (This time you will be facing the opposite direction.) Then hop on right foot to box (2), winding up on both feet again at parallel boxes (1). Another 180° turn to the right will bring you back into starting position, ready to repeat the pattern. The object is to complete the pattern as quickly and smoothly as possible. Begin slowly.

98. Long-Short Scramble

Emphasis: Footwork, Groundstroke
Skill level: Beginner, Intermediate, Advanced
Players/court: 2

Purpose: To develop quickness and agility.

Procedure: Player A at midcourt feeds a ball to B's forehand corner. B, at the baseline, moves to return the ball crosscourt. As soon as the first ball is hit, A feeds the second ball short to B's backhand. B runs to return the ball down-the-line. The next pattern starts with a deep ball to B's backhand corner, and the short ball to the forehand. Players rotate after five minutes.

NOTE—The feeder should make each shot challenging, but not impossible.

Variation: Eliminate the crosscourt and down-the-line placement for beginning players.

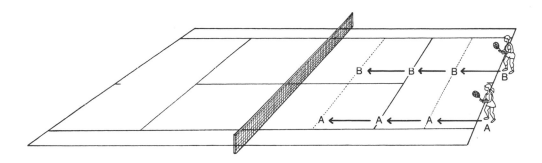

99. Split-Step Shadow Drill

Emphasis: Footwork
Skill level: Beginner, Intermediate
Players/court: 1 to Group

Purpose: To learn the split-step stop.

Procedure: Players start at the baseline. They run to an imaginary line midway between the baseline and the service line and come to a stop using the split step (a small jump landing on both feet simultaneously). After a momentary pause to see if they are in balance, the players run to the service line and stop, using the split step. This continues once more to an imaginary line midway between the service line and the net. This pattern is repeated five times.

NOTE—To be able to move in any direction, the player should be in balance before hitting the ball. When moving from the backcourt to the net, a split step can be used to gain balance, just before the opponent hits the ball. Any number of steps can precede the split step. The more time the player has before the opponent returns the ball, the more steps the player can take to get closer to the net.

100. Who Needs Strings?

Emphasis: Conditioning, Volley
Skill level: Intermediate, Advanced
Players/court: 2, 4, or 6

Purpose: To develop strength in the wrist and forearm of the racket hand.

Procedure: With covers on their rackets, A and B volley at the net, using the same strokes called for in match play. The added weight of the racket covers strengthens players' wrists and forearms.

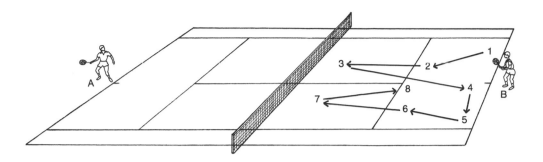

101. Eight Ball

Emphasis: Conditioning, Groundstroke, Volley, Overhead, Approach
Skill level: Intermediate, Advanced
Players/court: 2 to 6

Purpose: To practice hitting a variety of shots on the run.

Procedure: From the baseline Player A feeds eight balls to B as follows:
1. Deep into the forehand corner. B returns it deep down-the-line.
2. To forehand midcourt. B hits an approach shot deep down-the-line and moves to the net.
3. To the forehand. B volleys down-the-line.
4. A deep lob to the backcourt. B must run it down and return it after the bounce.
5. Deep into the backhand corner. B returns it deep down-the-line.
6. To the backhand midcourt. B hits an approach shot deep down-the-line and moves to the net.
7. To the backhand. B volleys down-the-line.
8. A short lob to the service line. B returns it with an overhead. Repeat pattern five times, then rotate players, B feeding balls to A.

Variations:
1. Player B hits all returns crosscourt.
2. Player B is not fed the next ball in the pattern unless the previous return lands in bounds. For example, if the forehand volley does not land in bounds, Player B must start over from the first forehand groundstroke.

102. Z Pattern

Emphasis: Conditioning, Footwork, Groundstroke, Volley, Overhead
Skill level: Intermediate, Advanced
Players/court: 2 to Group

Purpose: To develop quickness and agility, and to practice hitting the ball on the run.

Procedure: Player B stands at the baseline in the forehand corner. Player A, at midcourt, feeds five balls to B: the first to the backhand corner, the second to B's forehand at the service line, the third to the backhand inside the service court, and the fourth at the net for a forehand volley. The last ball is a lob to midcourt. B should sprint to return the five shots. The next pattern begins with B standing in the backhand corner, with the first ball hit to the forehand corner. After B completes the pattern six times (three starting in the forehand corner and three in the backhand corner), players rotate.

Variations:
1. More than two players may practice this drill, with the extra players waiting behind the baseline. After B finishes and leaves the court, C is ready to start. After each player completes two patterns, A joins the line and a new player feeds.
2. Targets may be set up for returns:
   - deep crosscourt
   - approach shot down-the-line
   - short crosscourt
   - angle volley
   - deep overhead.

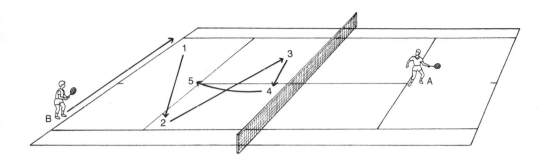

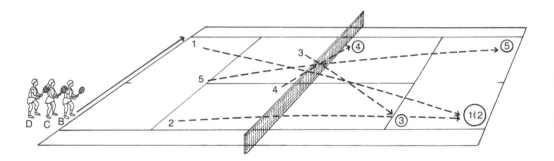

103. Volleyball Anyone?

Emphasis: Footwork
Skill level: Advanced
Players/court: 2 or 4

Purpose: To develop touch and control with the racket and improve foot mobility.

Procedure: Players A and B stand at the net. A feeds ball to B. B taps the ball to self and then volleys it across the net to A. A taps the ball to self and volleys the ball to B.

Variation: Initially, a forehand tap with a forehand volley, and a backhand tap with a backhand volley is the easiest. As the players improve, they might try a forehand tap across the body to a backhand volley, and the reverse.

Glossary

Alley—The area on each side of the court, between the singles and doubles sideline.

Angled shot—A ball hit on an extreme angle across the court.

Approach shot—A groundstroke that is followed to the net.

Backcourt—The area of the court between the baseline and midcourt (see diagram, p. ix).

Backhand court—The service court to the left of player.

Ball hopper—A basket used to collect and hold balls.

Baseline—The end boundary line of the court (see diagram, p. ix).

Carioca—A dance step used for improving footwork. When moving to the right, step to the side with the right foot, cross in front with the left foot, step to the side with the right, and cross behind with the left, etc.

Center mark—The mark at the center of the baseline (see diagram, p. ix).

Center service line—The line that divides the two service courts (see diagram, p. ix).

Crosscourt shot—A ball hit diagonally across the net from corner to corner.

Deep shot—A ball landing near the baseline.

Down-the-line—A ball hit parallel to and near a sideline.

Drive—A groundstroke hit with power.

Drop shot—A softly hit ball, with excessive backspin, that barely clears the net and bounces close to it.

Forecourt—The area of the court between the net and the midcourt (see diagram, p. ix).

Forehand court—The service court to the right of player.

Groundstroke—Stroke hit after the ball has bounced.

Half volley—Hitting the ball immediately after it bounces.

Lob—A ball hit high into the air, usually intended to go over the net player.

Midcourt—The area of the court a few feet to either side of the service line (see diagram, p. ix).

Overhead (smash)—A stroke hit overhead with a compact service motion. It may be taken in the air or after the bounce. The usual response to a lob.

Passing shot—A groundstroke attempting to pass beyond the reach of the net player.

Poach—The net player in doubles moves to the partner's side of the court to volley.

Rally—Hitting the ball back and forth over the net a number of times, in practice or in matches.

Serve (service)—The shot that starts a point.

Service court—The area of the court in which the service must land.

Service line—The back boundary line of the service court, (see diagram, p. ix).

Split-step stop (jump stop)—A small jump, landing on both feet simultaneously, to come to a stop. This is used when running from the backcourt to the forecourt to gain balance.

Volley—Hitting the ball before it bounces. This does not include the overhead motion.

CEDAR CREST COLLEGE LIBRARY

3 1543 50157 3697

796.342 P497t

Petro, Sharon.
The tennis drill book

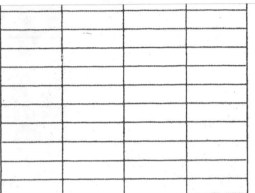

About t

Author S   eer. Currently as   s the first
woman   chaired
the Dep   's tennis
team fo   m for
three ye   lectures
on spor   of sports
at both

A highly   the
women'   her
seven-y   NCAA
Division   ving the
1985 se   Year.

Sharon   ity, her
master'   an University, and   me. She
has an avid interest in sports psychology and is currently pursuing a doctorate
in that field. Her leisure time pursuits include traveling, dancing, and reading.

Cressman Library
Cedar Crest College
Allentown, Pa. 18104

DEMCO